FOUNDATIONS OF PIANOFORTE TECHNIQUE

PREFACE

Most of the famous books of technical exercises were written 80 to 100 years ago. Though
cerned with playing the right note at the right time. A comprehensive technique requires mor
right note at the right time *in the right way*." It is because of the importance of the "right way"
tions as to 'how' and 'what to avoid.' Technical exercises are useless unless practised in the correct manner.

G. TANKARD,

Professor, Royal College of Music, London.
Examiner to the Associated Board of the Royal Schools
of Music.

How to Practise the Exercises

1. Learn them with the hands separately first.

2. Always play them rhythmically—i.e. with flow, not heavy accentuation.

3. Play them at three speeds; slow, medium and fast.

4. Play them at three tone levels; *p*, *mf*, *f*.

5. Sometimes play them also finger-staccato where practicable.

6. Always listen with deep-level concentration, especially to legato.

7. When you tire physically, stop, rest, shake the arms loosely and change the type of exercise.

8. Use all movements with control and economy.

9. Be as relaxed as possible, but do not flop or play lazily.

10. Keep the body, feet, head and shoulders still, but not rigid.

11. Do not beat time with the foot or head. Rhythm must be in the tone, not in the appearance.

12. It is better to practise one exercise twelve (or more) times than to play twelve exercises once each.

13. Watch the fingers as you play, but sometimes close the eyes.

14. Do not 'learn' the exercises and finish with them: they are in the nature of a 'daily dozen', to increase strength, independence and agility.

15. Make the exercises musical.

16. Play at two tone levels simultaneously, and listen to the softer one chiefly.

17. These exercises are graded from Grade II to Grade VIII. When they have been 'absorbed', move on to the more difficult exercises by Geoffrey Tankard and Eric Harrison in "Pianoforte Technique on an hour a day", which are graded from Grade VII to Concert level.

Order No: NOV 262587

FIVE-FINGER EXERCISES

Play each exercise 12 times: 4 times Andante *f*, 4 times Moderato *mf*, 4 times Allegro *mp*.

Hold the dotted note its *full* length.

Count 1 & 2 & 3 & 4 &

gentle nuances.

finger staccato.

finger-tips must be perpendicular.

Do not allow any *pp* note to miss.

E. & Co. 2587

Keep the finger-tips vertical into the keys.

Do not *roll* the hand. Let the 'weak' fingers
take the strain (Rotary exercises come later).

cantabile

Play with finger-tip from surface level.

dolce

echo

Do not raise the finger-tip more than ½ inch.

A little transferred weight in each finger-tip.

firmly

Keep the weaker side of the hand well poised.

Con bravura

Con grazia **Tempo giusto**

Do not rob the dotted note.

With a tight rhythm.

Draw the finger up as fast as possible, making the shortest contact with key.

Hands crossed over: master the separate hands first.

Do not squeeze the sustained note. Play the breve without sounding it, to aid the listening.

Rest the hand lightly on the sustained key.

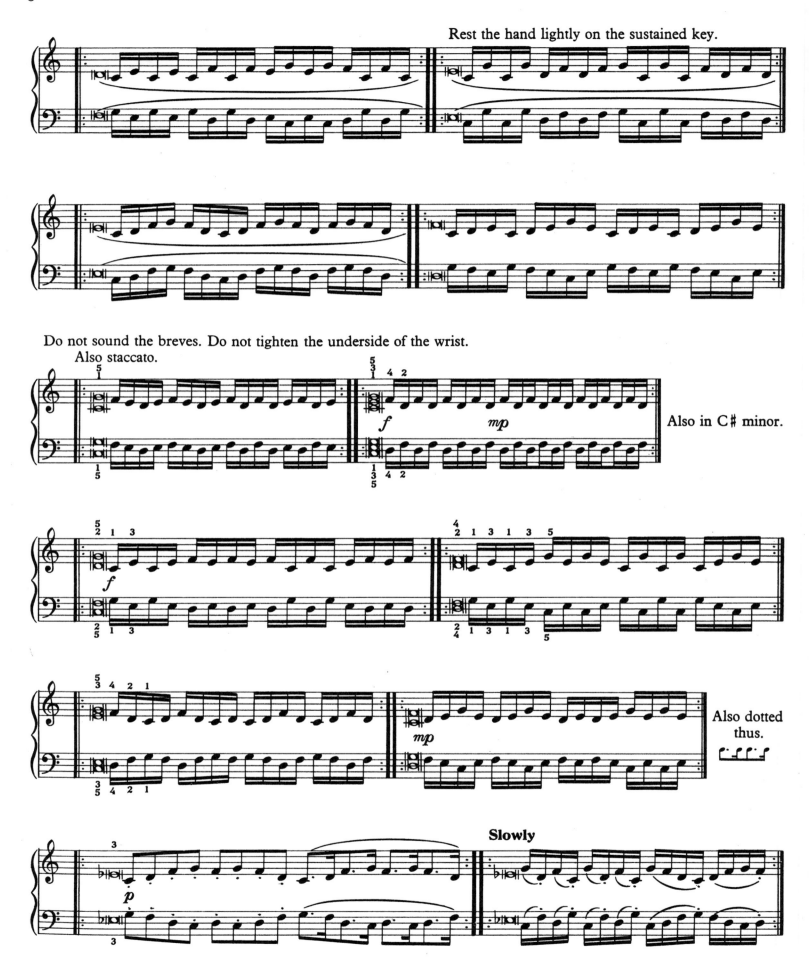

Do not sound the breves. Do not tighten the underside of the wrist.

Also staccato.

Also in C♯ minor.

Also dotted thus.

Slowly

Semiquavers lightly: crotchets cantabile.

Master the hands separately. *Watch* and listen.

Slowly and smoothly

Very slowly

Also bring out
the tenor, alto
or bass line.

Relax the elbows.

Lento

Keep the wrist loose but still.

Do not sway the forearm up and down. (It is easier but will not increase strength or finger independence).

Watch the action of the 5th finger. Finger-tips play vertically into the key.

Also in G minor.

Also in E♭ major. Also in D♭ major. Do not break any legato.

Shift neatly to new position.

etc. Also in $\left.\begin{matrix} D \\ A \\ G \end{matrix}\right\}$ major.

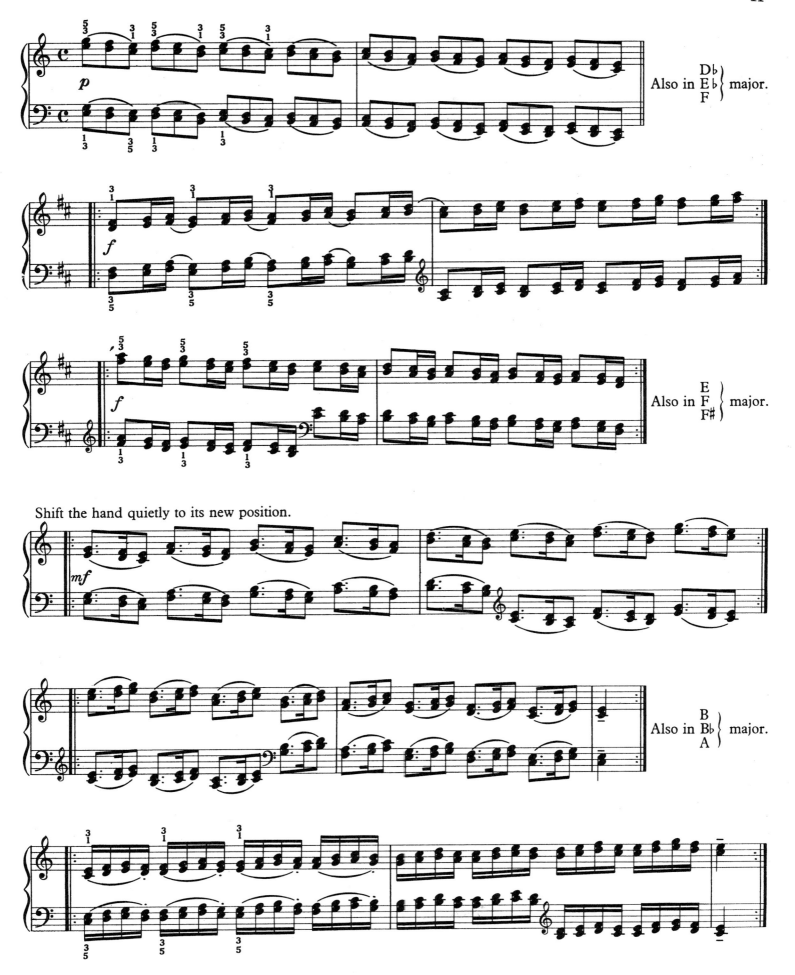

Also in $\left.\begin{array}{l} D\flat \\ E\flat \\ F \end{array}\right\}$ major.

Also in $\left.\begin{array}{l} E \\ F \\ F\sharp \end{array}\right\}$ major.

Shift the hand quietly to its new position.

Also in $\left.\begin{array}{l} B \\ B\flat \\ A \end{array}\right\}$ major.

Also in $\left.\begin{matrix} D\flat \\ E\flat \\ F \end{matrix}\right\}$ major.

Fine articulation, precise touch.

Scherzando

mp

To be played (a) from hand knuckles, (b) with slight up and down movements from wrist.

p   *cresc.*

f   *dim.*

Also in $\left.\begin{matrix} D \\ D\flat \end{matrix}\right\}$ major   Also in $\left.\begin{matrix} C \\ C\sharp \end{matrix}\right\}$ minor

E. & Co. 2587

Basic beat. A reliable basic beat is essential.
Count aloud, but count evenly and play to your counting—do *not* count to your playing.

Agility and definition.
2 octaves apart, continue to 4 octave range.

Also in D major.

Start an octave lower and continue to the top C of the piano.
Do not sustain 1st or 5th longer than proper duration.

Also in D♭ major.

Also in E♭ major.

Also in E major.

Also in A major.

Get an even quintuplet. Avoid

Also in D♭ major.

Also in G major.

Also in B♭ major.

Also in B major.

Also in D major.

Also in E♭ major.

THUMB EXERCISES

Develop a light, flexible independent thumb. Turn the elbow outwards, but keep it still and relaxed.

Do not twist, turn or roll the wrist. Let the thumb do its own work unaided.

Develop a musical thumb.

Use thumb independently (no rotation).

Thumb on each note, light staccato.

Also in D♭ / D / E♭ majors,   C / C♯ / E♭ minors

The thumb can be easily strained. Do not allow any pain to develop.

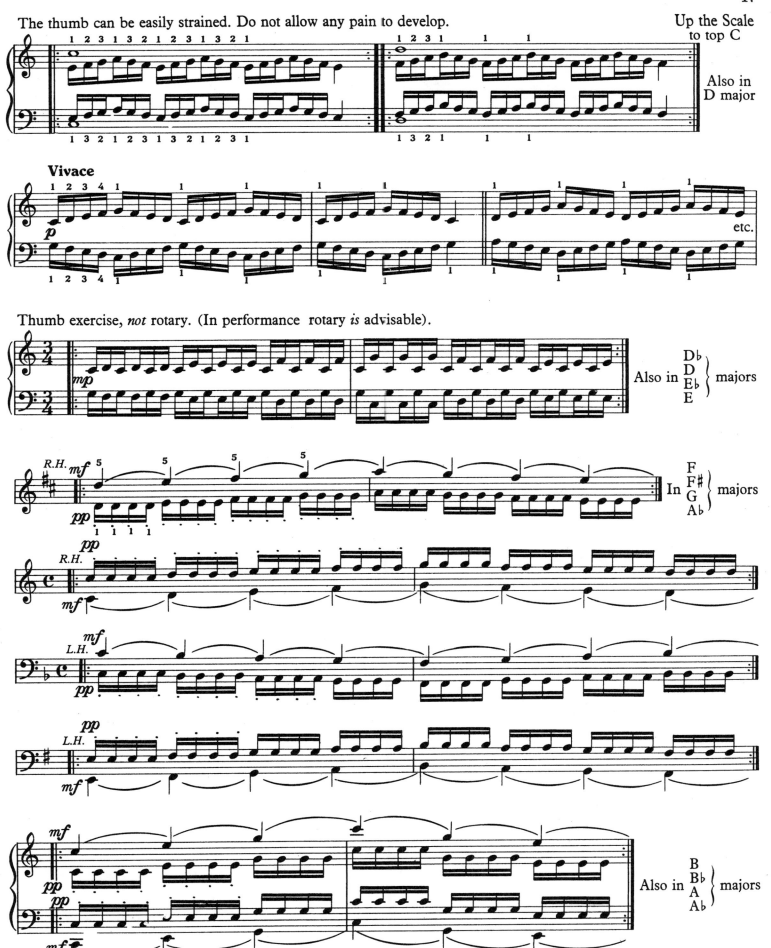

Also in
D major

Vivace

etc.

Thumb exercise, *not* rotary. (In performance rotary *is* advisable).

Also in D♭ D E♭ E } majors

In F F♯ G A♭ } majors

Also in B B♭ A A♭ } majors

REPEATED NOTES

A clean staccato. Make the last of the group as crisp as the others. With strong articulation.

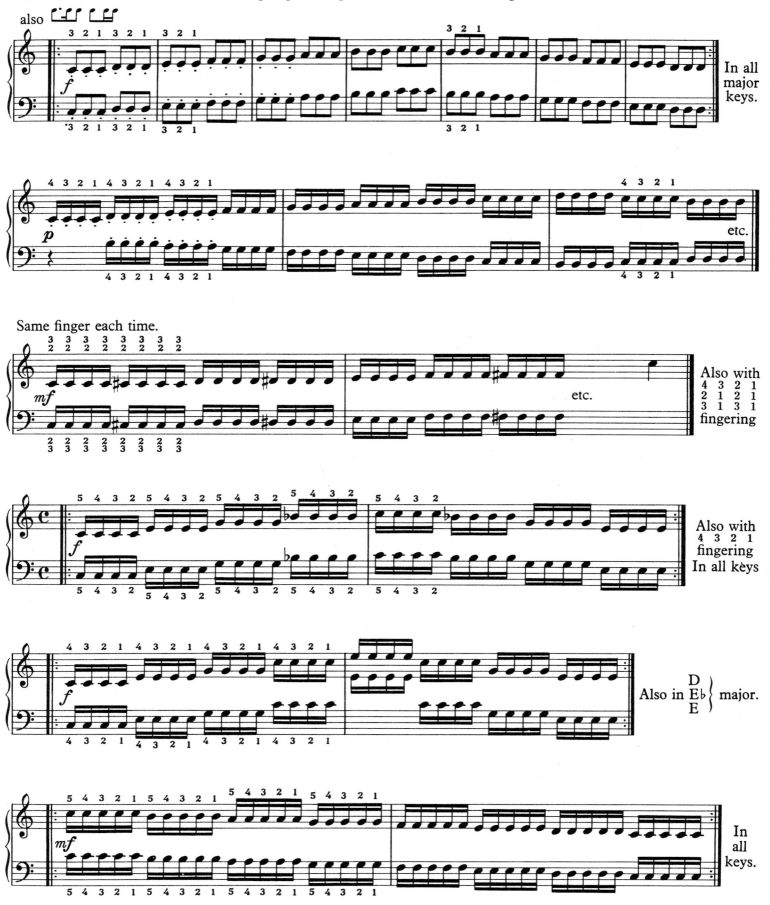

In all major keys.

etc.

Same finger each time.

Also with
4 3 2 1
2 1 2 1
3 1 3 1
fingering

etc.

Also with
4 3 2 1
fingering
In all keys

Also in E♭ } major.
D
E

In all keys.

ROTARY EXERCISES

Roll sideways from the elbow joint equally on both top and bottom notes.

Do not assist by finger adjustment: cover the keys carefully in advance.

Assist by finger-tip adjustment here.

Roll inwards.   Roll outwards.

Roll inwards.   Roll outwards.

Roll the hand slightly, but with control, into the finger-tips; avoid overlapping.
Lift the hand gracefully with a relaxed wrist.

ARPEGGIO EXERCISES

Bridge the gap carefully. Thumb under the hand.

Moderato

Hand over thumb.

And in $\left.\begin{array}{l}D \\ D\flat \\ E\flat \\ E\end{array}\right\}$ majors

in all keys
major and minor

Do not sustain thumb notes more than their correct value.

in all
white keys

Crossing hands

Legato—flowing

in all
white keys

LATERAL EXERCISES AND EXTENSIONS

in all keys.

in all keys.

in all keys.

Wheel round using the breve as a pivot.

Use as much lateral swing as you require, but no more.

The smaller the hand, the more movement is needed.

Swing gently up, then down. Relax on the quavers.

Moderato

mf

etc. through
all keys.

PHRASING AND INDEPENDENCE

Practise the hands separately until rhythmical and lyrical.

Make easy, graceful movements, the wrist relaxed.

Moderato

Master separate hands before putting together.

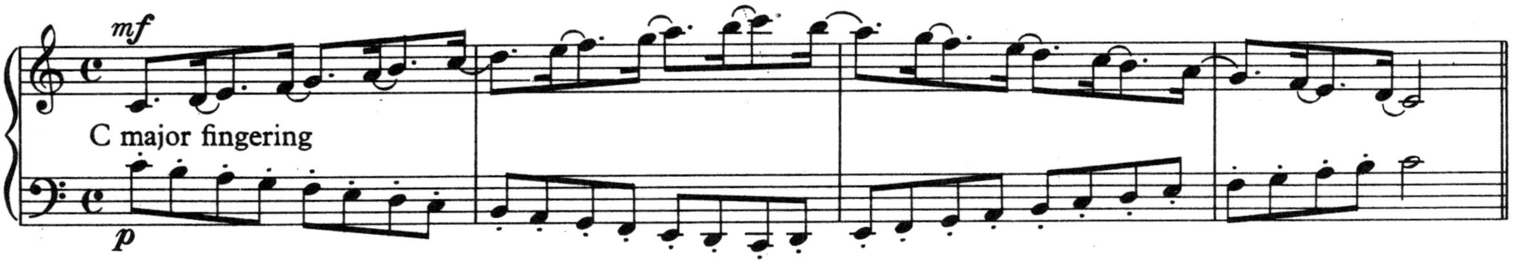

C major fingering

Bach. Invention in E major (2 Part)

WRIST STACCATO (OR HAND STACCATO)

Practise with full-wrist, half-wrist, and quarter-wrist movements and keep the elbow still.

Do not assist the wrist action with a complementary knuckle action.

etc.

Begin with the hand raised. Do not pluck the keys upwards.

leggiero

Crisp and clean.

TONE ASSESSMENT AND GRADATION

Think the sound *before* producing it.

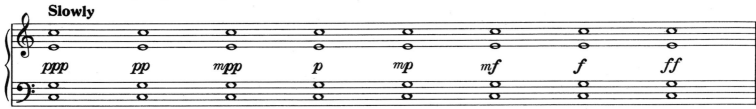

Ask for a definite sound volume. If you do not get it, try again.

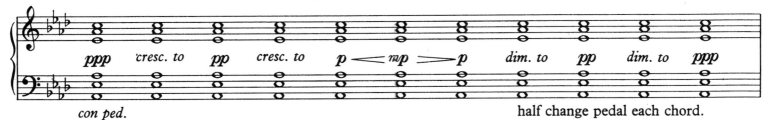

Sink smoothly into the sound. Think of getting richer and fuller (rather than louder).

The numbers 2-17 refer to shades of tone gradation, 2 is *pp*, 17 is *f*.

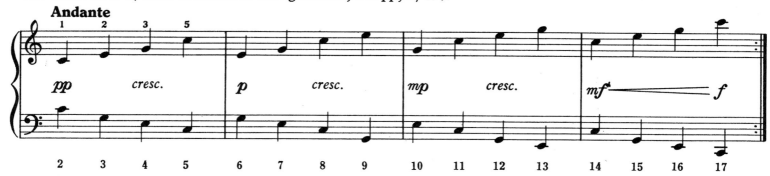

Learn to crescendo inside a diminuendo.

Portamento has a measurable length in every note. It is nearly legato.

Learn to diminish inside a crescendo

Expressiveness demands this; not *every* note gets progressively louder in a crescendo; if it did, there would be no natural flow of accentuation. The bars get proportionately louder, but up-beats and half-beats are usually lighter than down-beats—even in a crescendo (unless *very* steep, e.g. *p* to *f* in one bar).

Portamento touch is long, not short, like a sigh, āh, āh, āh, āh, or like the instrusive 'h' to a singer. The effect should be pathetic, not happy. Think of Mozart's slow movements.

COMBINED RHYTHMS

First establish a firm beat. Then play the hands separately. When assured, combine the parts.

5 against 4

4 against 5

Do not be discouraged by the mathematical complications of 5 against 6. Practise the hands separately until the muscular memory takes over from 'thinking'.

5 against 6

6 against 5

Use normal fingering of C major.
3 against 2

PEDAL EXERCISES

Legato (or syncopated) pedalling. Count aloud; slow beat; middle finger only.

Pedal goes down on the second beat, off *precisely* on the first.

Direct pedalling (i.e. *on* the beat).

The art of pedalling is subtle and cannot be mastered by exercises. Direct pedalling is easy: the pedal goes down *on* the beat, therefore comes off *before* it. In using direct pedal do not use undue foot or leg pressure: pedal lightly and silently: never hit the pedal or shake the mechanism. Heels must be on the floor; if necessary sit on the edge of the stool. The weight must be on the heel, never on the sole. If the legs are not long enough to rest the weight of the lower leg on the heel, the pedal must *never* be used. Nobody under 4 ft. 6 ins. must touch the pedal. No child under grade 3 should be allowed to touch the pedal, unless he is specially gifted.

In legato pedalling make sure the previous chord never gets into the next chord. The golden rule is to listen for harmonic purity combined with harmonic smoothness.

E. & Co. 2587

Half-pedal means changing the foot very quickly so that it only does half its work of damping. If the foot is changed quickly it will damp the higher and shorter strings, whilst only slightly damping the lower and longer ones.

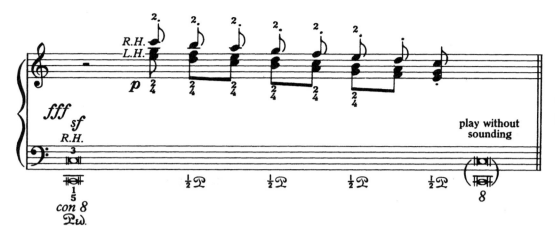

The bass should still be sounding but the treble strings silenced.

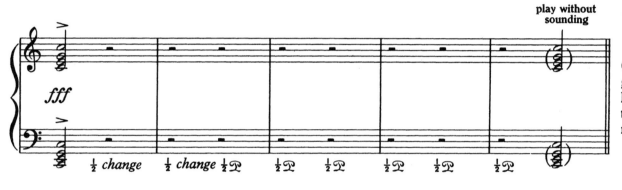

On a first class concert grand it is possible to half-change up to 30 times without stopping resonance completely.

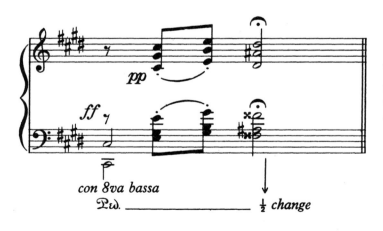

This half-change should damp the *pp* chords in Rachmaninoff's C♯ min. Prelude whilst retaining the bass *ff* notes.

Half-*damping* (rare) is a musical-box effect, which can be used in delicate music (often in Debussy). The weight of the dampers is half-released from the strings by a very gentle foot pressure. This half-mutes the strings, giving a slight 'hang-over' effect. It is condemned by many responsible teachers and pianists, but there *are* experienced teachers who use and teach it effectively.

Published by Novello Publishing Limited
Printed in Great Britain

E. & Co. 2587